I0480148

100 Quote Prompts

2020 Edition

Written by Jaz Johnson

Edited by Jaz Johnson & Brandon Tate

Formatted by Jaz Johnson

Cover Design by Jaz Johnson

First paperback edition published January 1st, 2020.

ISBN: 978-1-951626-04-4 (e-book)

ISBN: 978-1-951626-05-1 (paperback)

Published by TC Studios LLC

www.TCStudiosHQ.com

Table of Contents

Introductions

Hello! Welcome to our 2020 edition of *100 Quote Prompts*. This book is a part of our creative group, **Prompt Party**. It's going to get your creative mojo flowing and make you want to start creating!

This book includes the following:

1. 100 prompts in eight different mediums (a), eight different genres (b), and ten different themes (c).
   a. Pencil (P), Color Pencil (CP), Acrylic Paint (AP), Marker (M), Crayon (C), Gouache (G), Watercolor (W), and Ink (I).
   b. Fantasy (F), Science Fiction (SF), Romance (R), Horror (H), Dystopian (D), Slice of Life (SL), Action & Adventure (AA), and Mystery (M).
   c. Fear, Anger, Love, Sorrow, Threatening, Shock, Confused, Hopeful, Desperate, and Betrayal.
2. 10 drawing exercises – one for each theme.
3. 10 writing exercises – one for each theme.

How To Use Our Prompts

Each prompt will list a hypothetical situation and a few suggested mediums to draw with, as well as suggested paths you can take with the prompt. You are **not** required to use the mediums listed, or to use the brainstorming sections. They are **only suggestions**.

Some prompts talk about you, but you don't always have to draw/write yourself. You can make up a character, or characters, too!

The goal is to draw or write a piece of work using the prompts provided. How you get there is ultimately up to you.

Share Your Work & Tag Us

We would love to be able to see the amazing things you come up with and tell you how much we love them!

To do that, all you have to do is post your work to Facebook, Instagram, or Twitter and tag us @PromptParty. Then we'll be able to see, share, and comment on them.

Submit To Our Anthologies

Would you like your work to be published? People are using our prompt books across the country, and many of them are submitting their work to our annual anthologies.

An anthology is a collection of work by many different people. Each year, we publish several with work made using our various prompt books.

The authors and artists of the published submissions receive shared 25% royalties (must be 18+), and 10% goes back into helping communities like yours. This money goes towards public school donations, public library donations, and more. So, help your community out by getting more people involved!

For more details on royalties and our mission to give back to communities across the country, visit our website, www.TCStudiosHQ.com.

To submit your work to our anthology, please do the following:

- Send an email to submissions@tcstudioshq.com with the following:
  - **Subject Line:**
    - 100 Quote Prompts Anthology Submission (2020)
  - **Body:**
    - First and last name (or pen/artist name).
    - The genre/medium you used.
  - **Attachments:**
    - Attached work.
      - Attached as a **PDF** for literature.
      - Attached as a **PNG** for art.
    - Attached signed publication form.
      - You can find this on our website.

If you are selected, we will reach out to you to request more information.

For more information on our other anthologies and an in-depth guide on how to submit to them, visit our website, www.TCStuidiosHQ.com.

Check Out Our Work

Did you know that we also publish novels, comics, and other creative guides?

To find out more about everything we publish and where you can read/get them, visit our website, www.TCStudiosHQ.com.

Chapter One: Fear.

#1 – "Did you hear that?" (H) | (CP) (I) (M)

Brainstorm (Writing) …

- Where might they be that they're hearing something suspicious?
    - What might the environment be like?
    - Why are they there to begin with?
- What might that noise be?
    - Should they be running from it?
    - Could it be a misunderstanding?
    - What does the noise sound like?

Brainstorm (Drawing) …

- Think of a person's body language when they're scared.
    - Are they looking around? Are they frozen in place?
- What might their facial expressions be?
    - Are their eyes tearing?
    - Are their teeth chattering?
- Again, where might they be that they're so spooked?
    - What is the environment like?

Writing Exercise #1

Write an exaggerated scene of you facing one of your fears.

7

#2 – "What are those things?!" (F) (H) | (P) (G) (AP)

Brainstorm (Writing) …

- What situation are they in that they would come across unknown creatures?
- Is it actually an unknown creature, or perhaps something mundane – like exaggerated shadows?
- Does the creature have any reaction to being discovered?
  - Is it scared? Defensive? Affectionate?
- Is it even a creature at all?
  - What else might it be?
    - A new piece of technology? A terribly outdated pair of shoes?

Brainstorm (Drawing) …

- Have fun creating a creature of your own!
  - Is it terrifying? Is it mythical? Is it downright adorable?
- Remember to think about expression.
  - Are they pointing at the unknown?
  - Are they cowering from it?
  - Are they hovering over it with interest?
- Where did they find it?
- If it's not a creature, what might it be?
  - What might be the situation surrounding this question?

You can share your work with us on Facebook, Instagram & Twitter!

Tag us @PromptParty and use #PromptParty.

We'd love to see what you come up with!

#3 – "They're … They're coming for us." (AA) (H) (D) | (W) (M) (C)

Brainstorm (Writing) …

- What or who is coming for them?
  - How long do they have before they arrive?
  - What plans or actions need to be put in place?
- Why are they being pursued?
  - What have they done, if anything at all?
  - Has someone been wrongly accused?
  - Are they being chased for sport?

Brainstorm (Drawing) …

- What do you picture is coming for them?
  - Draw the person or persons – or creatures? Or whatever! – that's coming for these characters.
- What condition are the characters in who are being pursued?
  - Have they been on the run?
  - Is this information new to them?
  - Are they somewhere safe?
    - Do they need to get somewhere safe?

Do you want your work published?

You can submit any work made using our prompts to our annual anthologies! Published submissions receive shared 25% royalties.

You can find more information on our website, www.TCStudiosHQ.com.

#4 – "Please …No … No!" (H) (SL) | (I) (P) (CP)

Brainstorm (Writing) …

- What don't they want to happen?
  - Are they doing anything other than talking to try to stop it?
  - What or who is causing the unwanted action?
    - Why is it causing this character so much discomfort?
    - How might they have found themselves in this situation?
  - Create a list of possible scenarios, ranging from severe to mundane.
    - Example: A threat of murder – in reality or through a TV screen.

Brainstorm (Drawing) …

- Play around with perspective.
  - Maybe their hand is reaching out towards the viewer.
  - Maybe they are looking up at their assailant, or have an arm outstretched towards who/what they are trying to stop.

Did you know?

A percentage of every anthology sold goes towards helping communities like yours. This includes donations to charities, funding of scholarships, creating of programs, and more!

You can find more information on our website, www.TCStudiosHQ.com.

#5 – "What have I done?" (R) (SL) | (G) (W) (C)

Brainstorm (Writing) …

- Think about the emotion this person must be feeling.
  - The question implies regret. But to what magnitude?
    - Did they realize a mistake they've made at work? Or have they just caused someone's untimely demise?
- What *have* they done?
  - What comes to mind when you picture a character saying this?
  - What are the circumstances surrounding this question?
- Are there witnesses to the regrettable act?
  - How might they feel about what's happening/happened?

Brainstorm (Drawing) …

- Think about the scenery of this moment.
  - Where is this person?
  - Are they with anyone else?
  - What might be around them that could help tell the story of what just happened?
- Think about the character's emotion.
  - Are they scared? Angry? How can you show that?

Did you know?

In addition to our annual prompt anthologies, every year we have themed anthologies that you can also submit to!

You can find more information on our website, www.TCStudiosHQ.com.

#6 – "Are they dead?" (SF) (H) | (C) (AP) (I)

Brainstorm (Writing) …

- How could they not know if a person is dead?
    - How is the body positioned?
    - Are their eyes open? Closed?
    - Is there any smell? Any blood?
- Play around with the tone of voice.
    - Maybe this is being said seriously.
    - Maybe someone is a comically heavy sleeper.
- Where could this be taking place?
- Who is asking the question?
    - The police? A wandering group of friends? A nurse?

Brainstorm (Drawing) …

- Where could this be taking place?
    - A hospital? Out in the woods? A hotel room?
    - Play around with how and where this scene could play out.
- How might a body look when it's mistaken to be/dead?
    - Things to think about:
        - Color.
        - Texture.
        - Perspective.

Drawing Exercise #1

Draw a comical version of something you fear.

#7 – "What am I supposed to do, now?!" (SL) (AA) | (M) (CP) (P)

Brainstorm (Writing) …

- Why is this person so panicked?
    - What happened to make them feel like they're out of options?
    - How does their personality play into feeling helpless?
- Are they at fault for the situation they're in?
    - What might they have done?
    - Is anyone else involved in the situation?

Brainstorm (Drawing) …

- Think of a person's facial structure when they're yelling.
    - Play around with its exaggeration.
        - Is there any sadness in their anger?
        - See if you can mix emotions in their expression.
- How can you express desperation in this character's body language?
    - Where are their hands? How are they positioned?
    - Is their back curved or arched?

Looking for a challenge?

Try doing one of our prompts with your friend(s)! See if you can come up with something together.

#8 – "There's someone in the house." (H) (M) | (G) (W) (AP)

Brainstorm (Writing) …

- Who is saying this?
    - A Child? Spouse?
    - Think about how the tone of the information could change based on who is saying it.
    - Think of how the reaction of the person being told could change based on who is telling them.
- What might their response be?
    - Cowardly? Defensive? Cautious?
    - What might they do in response?
        - Investigate on their own?
        - Call the police?

Brainstorm (Drawing) …

- Think of the atmosphere of this situation.
    - Warped perspective can make a scene more intense.
    - How could your color palette change the mood?
    - Adding texture to shading can make a scene more vibrant.

Did you know?

We also make books to help with storytelling. With help on things like creating characters, world-building, magic systems, and more!

You can find more information on our website, www.TCStudiosHQ.com.

#9 – "We're not alone." (H) | (C) (I) (M)

Brainstorm (Writing) …

- What could this mean?
    - Is a romantic moment being intruded upon?
    - Is someone lurking about?
    - Is someone sharing a touching moment?
- Think about the context of this statement and play around with how this scene could go.

Brainstorm (Drawing) …

- What might the situation surrounding this statement look like?
- Are they having a heart to heart?
    - Is it somewhere romantic?
- Are they fearful?
    - Is it somewhere scary?
- Think about how the location could change the tone and meaning of this statement.

Did you know?

We also publish novels and comics that you can read!

You can find more information on our website, www.TCStudiosHQ.com.

#10 – "Get it off, get it off!" (SL) | (P) (G) (W)

Brainstorm (Writing) …

- What are they trying to get off of them?
  - A bug? Slime? Some ungodly creature?
- How did it get on them in the first place?
  - Did they walk into a spider-web? A mysterious cave?
- What might happen if they don't get it off in a timely fashion?
  - Will it give them a poisonous bite?
  - Will it burn through their clothing? Their skin?

Brainstorm (Drawing) …

- Think about how you can set up your figures.
  - Play around with overlapping figures.
  - Use three elements:
    - The person with something on them.
    - The thing/substance that's on them.
    - The person trying/coming to get it off.
  - Try your best to capture the panic in their body language.

Do you want to give us a prompt for next year's edition?

You can submit prompt ideas you have based on next year's chapter themes. Credit will be given if selected.

You can find more information on our website, www.TCStudiosHQ.com.

Chapter Two: Anger.

#11 – "Don't you dare." (SL) | (P) (I) (G)

Brainstorm (Writing) …

- What is about to happen?
    - What could be making this character so upset about it?
    - What position is the person about to do the action in?
        - Is it blackmail?
        - An action of spite?
        - Is it meant to challenge them? Tease them?

Brainstorm (Drawing) …

- How might this person's emotion affect their body language?
    - Are they pointing a finger?
    - Are their hands clenched into fists?
    - Are they covering their mouth in shock?
- Play around with expression and see how it can affect the tone of the statement.

Writing Exercise #2

Write out a scene of pure fury.
Show, don't tell.

#12 – "I'll kill you!" (H) (AA) | (CP) (C) (W)

Brainstorm (Writing) …

- Think about the context of this statement.
  - Is it said in anger? In jest?
  - How could this cause problems in the plot?
- Perhaps a police officer is using this, said in jest, as evidence in a case against the character for murder, for which they did not commit.
- If it's said in earnest, what might the situation around that statement look like?
  - Is it being said during an attempt?
  - Is it said in warning?
  - Why is it being said in the first place?
  - What is the reaction of the person it's being said to?

Brainstorm (Drawing) …

- Here's a good chance to play around with exaggeration.
  - Try an angry expression.
  - Try a playful expression.
- Is someone being chased?
  - Think about cartoon chase scenes. Try to imitate them.
- It could be a serious scene, too.
  - How dire is the situation?

Did you know?

We post daily writing & drawing prompts on our Social Medias for everyone to participate in.

Find us @PromptParty and use #PromptParty.

You can find more information on our website, www.TCStudiosHQ.com.

#13 – "You've got some nerve." (SL) | (M) (AP) (G)

Brainstorm (Writing) …

- What's being done?
    - Has someone just stepped out of line?
    - Is someone being threatened?
    - What kind of circumstances could involve this statement?
- Explore the emotions of both parties – the offended and the offender.
    - How do their emotions play off one another?
    - Are they both malicious? Could one party be regretful?

Brainstorm (Drawing) …

- Try to capture the emotions of both parties.
    - How are they standing/sitting?
    - How can you show how they feel towards one another?

Did you know?

In addition to posting daily on Social Media, we have daily interactive posts on our YouTube channel, Podcast, and Blog.

You can find more information on our website, www.TCStudiosHQ.com.

#14 – "How dare you." (SL) (F) | (I) (W) (P)

Brainstorm (Writing) …

- How has this person been offended?
  - Did it come from a stranger?
  - Someone they know/knew?
  - What might this person do in response?
- Describe the offender.
  - How do they feel about what they're doing?
  - Was it planned?
  - What are their next steps?

Brainstorm (Drawing) …

- Play around with using shading techniques to highlight expressions.
  - You can include:
    - Hatching.
    - Cross-hatching.
    - Stippling.
    - Contour Lines.
    - Scribbles.

You can share your work with us on Facebook, Instagram & Twitter!

Tag us @PromptParty and use #PromptParty.

We'd love to see what you come up with!

#15 – "Fuck off!" (SL) (AA) | (C) (CP) (M)

Brainstorm (Writing) ...

- Boom!
    - Was there a straw that broke the camel's back?
    - Is someone just having a bad day?
    - Was this a reaction to someone or something?
- Is there a response from the person being yelled at?
    - Is there going to be a fight?
    - How can they deescalate the situation?
    - Will a third party get involved?
        - Was the outburst *caused* by the third party?

Brainstorm (Drawing) ...

- How could you express this without using words?
    - Flipping the bird?
    - A person's facial expression?
    - An image on a T-shirt?
    - Play around with how you can show this.

Do you want your work published?

You can submit any work made using our prompts to our annual anthologies! Published submissions receive shared 25% royalties.

You can find more information on our website, www.TCStudiosHQ.com.

#16 – "You're nothing but a liar!" (R) (SL) | (AP) (P) (W)

Brainstorm (Writing) …

- What were they lying about?
- Were they telling the truth this time?
- What has this person tolerated?
  - What were they lied to about before?
  - What are they accusing someone of lying about, now?
- *Did* the person lie?
  - If yes, are they sorry about it?
  - If no, what could they do to prove that they're not lying?
- How could the situation go?
  - If they *are* lying, what might the accuser do?

Brainstorm (Drawing) …

- What kind of scene could match this statement?
  - Did someone walk in on their spouse cheating?
  - Have they presented pictures/facts to prove something?
  - Are they simply in denial about something?
- Think about their environment.
  - Is this being said publicly?
    - Are there people around to react?
  - Is this being said in private?
    - How could it escalate?

Drawing Exercise #2

Practice expressing anger in both facial and body language.

#17 – "You're a monster!" (SF) | (M) (I) (CP)

Brainstorm (Writing) …

- Is this being said literally or figuratively?
  - If literal, did something happen to create a monster?
    - An experiment gone wrong?
  - If figurative, what could the accused have done that was so monstrous?
- What are the perspectives of either parties?
  - The accuser – are they afraid? Angry?
  - The accused – are they offended? Afraid? Indifferent?

Brainstorm (Drawing) …

- Draw this from the perspective of the accused.
- Is this a literal statement?
  - Are they being ostracized?
  - Are they afraid? Aggressive?
  - What might the monster look like?
- Is this a figurative statement?
  - How do they feel about the accusation?
    - Offended? Indifferent? Proud?

Did you know?

A percentage of every anthology sold goes towards helping communities like yours. This includes donations to charities, funding of scholarships, creating of programs, and more!

You can find more information on our website, www.TCStudiosHQ.com.

#18 – "We can't just sit here and do nothing." (AA) (D) | (G) (C) (W)

Brainstorm (Writing) …

- What's happening that needs a response from them?
    - War? Crime? Crisis?
- Who are the ones that need to respond?
    - Civilians? Warriors? Criminals?
- Where might this be taking place?
    - Is there something stopping them from responding?

Brainstorm (Drawing) …

- Try to express the tension of the situation.
    - The person saying the statement.
    - Those they are saying it to.
- Where might this be taking place?
    - Is there something stopping them from responding?
    - Illustrate where/what that might be.

Did you know?

In addition to our annual prompt anthologies, every year we have
<u>themed</u> anthologies that you can also submit to!

You can find more information on our website,
www.TCStudiosHQ.com.

#19 – "Just who do you think you are?" (SL) (M) | (AP) (M) (I)

Brainstorm (Writing) …

- Is someone doing something out of line?
    - Someone with a known title?
        - Is it famous or infamous?
    - Perhaps an imposter?
    - Or maybe it's just some jerk.
- What's being done to get this response?
    - Is someone being insulted?
    - Did a customer's coupon expire?
    - Did someone steal a parking spot?

Brainstorm (Drawing) …

- How could this scene be set up?
- Think about the kind of people on either end.
    - Does the accuser or the accused have any authority?
    - How does one party feel towards the other?
        - How can you illustrate those feelings?

Looking for a challenge?

Try doing one of our prompts with your friend(s)! See if you can
come up with something together.

#20 – "What the hell's going on here?!" (SL) (M) (SF) | (CP) (P) (W)

Brainstorm (Writing) …

- What *is* in fact going on?
  - Come up with a list of scenarios that could justify this response.
- What context might be surrounding the situation?
  - Is it intimate?
  - Is it motherly?
  - Is it a reaction to a surprising moment during a favorite book/TV show?

Brainstorm (Drawing) …

- What tone could you set this scene up with?
  - Comical? Serious? Curious?
  - Play around with how you can set the stage.

Did you know?

We also make books to help with storytelling. With help on things like creating characters, world-building, magic systems, and more!

You can find more information on our website, www.TCStudiosHQ.com.

Chapter Three: Love.

#21 – "You're everything I've ever wanted." (R) | (AP) (CP) (M)

Brainstorm (Writing) …

- What could that mean for someone?
    - What traits could encompass someone's perfect partner?
    - See if you can show that, not tell.

Brainstorm (Drawing) …

- Experiment:
    - Try drawing a montage of ideal traits this person sees in someone.
    - Maybe shown as thought/memory bubbles above their head.

Writing Exercise #3

Write about the first time you fell in love, or what you think falling in love would be like.

#22 – "Please come home." (R) (D) | (W) (G) (I)

Brainstorm (Writing) …

- Why isn't the person home?
    - Are they upset in their relationship?
    - Did a child run away?
    - Are they out exploring space? New lands?
- What's happening at home without them?
    - Are they in danger?
    - Are they lonely?
- Is there a reason that person can't come home?
    - Are they on the run?
    - Have they been captured?

Brainstorm (Drawing) …

- Choose a perspective to illustrate.
- The person away from home:
    - Are they reading a letter from their loved one?
    - Where are they reading it?
    - Do they want to go home?
- The person wanting them to come home:
    - Are they talking on the phone? Writing a letter? Praying?
    - Are they upset? Sad? Desperate?

Did you know?

We also publish novels and comics that you can read!

You can find more information on our website,
www.TCStudiosHQ.com.

#23 – "Everyone makes sacrifices." (SL) (AA) | (C) (P) (AP)

Brainstorm (Writing) …

- Who is saying this, and who is it being said to?
  - A commander to a soldier?
  - A mentor to a student?
  - A parent to a child?
- How could who's saying this change the context and situation surrounding the statement?

Brainstorm (Drawing) …

- Try to capture the potential intensity of the conversation taking place.
  - How might you do that?
    - Consider your color palette.
    - Consider your shading.
    - Consider your figure placement.

Do you want to give us a prompt for next year's edition?

You can submit prompt ideas you have based on next year's chapter themes. Credit will be given if selected.

You can find more information on our website, www.TCStudiosHQ.com.

#24 – "I'll always be there for you." (R) | (CP) (G) (M)

Brainstorm (Writing) …

- What might be going on in someone's life that they'd need to hear this?
  - What conversation might have come before or after this statement?
  - What might being there for this person mean?
  - How can you show the bond these characters have?
    - Think about their body languages – how they interact with each other.
    - What in their surroundings show the progress in their relationship?

Brainstorm (Drawing) …

- Try illustrating a collage of photos that show this relationship.

Did you know?

We post daily writing & drawing prompts on our Social Medias for everyone to participate in.

Find us @PromptParty and use #PromptParty.

You can find more information on our website, www.TCStudiosHQ.com.

#25 – "I'm sure they're watching over us." (SL) (H) | (W) (C) (AP)

Brainstorm (Writing) ...

- Who are "they"?
    - o Is it implied that they've passed away?
    - o Are they literally able to look over them?
- How would that be possible?
    - o Are they being monitored?
- What is the tone of voice for this?
    - o Are they wary?
    - o Are they relieved?
    - o Are they sentimental?

Brainstorm (Drawing) ...

- Think about the tone of voice that might be used for this statement.
    - o How might that translate to your illustration?
    - o How might it effect the environment the characters are in?

Did you know?

In addition to posting daily on Social Media, we have daily interactive posts on our YouTube channel, Podcast, and Blog.

You can find more information on our website, www.TCStudiosHQ.com.

#26 – "I love you." (R) | (M) (I) (P)

Brainstorm (Writing) …

- What might be happening around this statement?
  - Is it a confession?
  - Is it a final farewell?
- What might the reaction to it be?
  - Happy? Remorseful?

Brainstorm (Drawing) …

- Think about the emotion between these characters.
  - What if it's a confession?
  - What if it's a farewell?
- What might be the surroundings be like?
  - Are they in the midst of chaos?
  - Are they in private amongst themselves?

Drawing Exercise #3

Draw a tender scene between two lovers.

#27 – "It's my passion." (SL) | (G) (CP) (C)

Brainstorm (Writing) …

- What are they passionate about?
    - ○ What might it cause them to do?
    - ○ How might it cause them to act?
    - ○ How does it affect their lifestyle?

Brainstorm (Drawing) …

- Illustrate someone living their passion.
    - ○ What might their home look like?
        - ▪ Showcase bits of their passion around their space.

You can share your work with us on Facebook, Instagram & Twitter!

Tag us @PromptParty and use #PromptParty.

We'd love to see what you come up with!

#28 – "This isn't love!" (R) (D) | (AP) (W) (I)

Brainstorm (Writing) …

- Is it heartbreak? Is it abuse?
    - How long might they have been holding that statement back?
    - What made them come forward with how they felt?
- Is someone trying to convince someone they care about regarding a toxic relationship?
    - Why are they stepping forward?
        - How many times have they tried before?

Brainstorm (Drawing) …

- Think about the scene that the above brainstorming might paint.
- Is one or more party crying?
    - What might their body language be?
        - Are they backing away in fear?
        - Are they shaking their friend's shoulders? Showing them proof? Warning signs?

Do you want your work published?

You can submit any work made using our prompts to our annual anthologies! Published submissions receive shared 25% royalties.

You can find more information on our website, www.TCStudiosHQ.com.

#29 – "There's nothing I wouldn't do for my child." (SL) (AA) (SF) | (M) (CP) (P)

Brainstorm (Writing) …

- What is this parent prepared to do?
  - Fight? Steal? Kill?
- What are the circumstances that are pushing them to prepare for drastic measures?
  - Has their child been kidnapped?
  - Are they being blackmailed?
  - Are they trying to keep their child unaware of their dangerous profession?
    - Is that how they provide for their family? What is their profession?

Brainstorm (Drawing) …

- Illustrate a determined parent handling their business for their child – however that takes place.
  - It could be helping them out of a tough spot.
  - Maybe it's answering their call while working their dangerous job.

Did you know?

A percentage of every anthology sold goes towards helping communities like yours. This includes donations to charities, funding of scholarships, creating of programs, and more!

You can find more information on our website, www.TCStudiosHQ.com.

#30 – "They … told me they loved me." (R) (SL) | (P) (G) (I)

Brainstorm (Writing) …

- This seems like it was said in shock. But how so?
- Are they surprised, yet share the same feelings?
- Are they surprised, because they've just been betrayed?
- Think about the context of the statement and how you can weave a story around it.
    - Are they descending into sorrow?
    - Are they slowly filling with joy?

Brainstorm (Drawing) …

- How might that confession, or realization, effect the set-up of your image?
    - Think about their body language and/or facial expression.
    - How might props help tell the story?
        - Are they holding a bouquet? A stack of divorce papers?

Did you know?

In addition to our annual prompt anthologies, every year we have <u>themed</u> anthologies that you can also submit to!

You can find more information on our website, www.TCStudiosHQ.com.

Chapter Four: Sorrow.

#31 – "Please … Make it stop." (SF) (D) | (I) (G) (AP)

Brainstorm (Writing) …

- What could be happening to this character to make them so distraught?
  - o Are they being tortured?
  - o Are they receiving a painful medical treatment?
  - o Are they in emotional pain?
- Who might be on the other side of this?
  - o How do they feel about the pain that this person is experiencing?
- What might this character do in desperation to make the action/experience stop?

Brainstorm (Drawing) …

- Think about how you can capitalize on the intensity of this scene.
  - o How might you position this character to emphasize their discomfort?
  - o Think about the situation that might be surrounding this statement, as mentioned above.
  - o Play around with your set up to reflect the situation.

Writing Exercise #4

Write about someone who has just lost someone/something dear to them.

#32 – "How can they do this to us?" (D) (AA) | (CP) (M) (C)

Brainstorm (Writing) …

- Think about the background of this question.
- Who are they talking about?
    - The government – "keeping them down"?
    - Parents – did they get grounded?
    - Teacher – Did they give them a ton of homework?
- What is the emotion behind this question?

Brainstorm (Drawing) …

- Dramatize the asking of this question.
- Use props and the character's environment to show what's being done to them.
    - What items could show what's going on?
    - What location could give a hint to what's going on?

Looking for a challenge?

Try doing one of our prompts with your friend(s)! See if you can come up with something together.

#33 – "We can't just let them die out there." (F) (AA) | (P) (W) (I)

Brainstorm (Writing) …

- Who are they talking about?
  - Soldiers?
  - Animals?
  - Civilians?
- Are they planning on doing anything to stop that from happening?
  - If so, what?
  - What/who would that entail?

Brainstorm (Drawing) …

- Try drawing what might be going on around these characters.
  - Is it a battlefield?
  - Is it a natural disaster?
  - Experiment with how you can set up the context of this statement.

Did you know?

We also make books to help with storytelling. With help on things like creating characters, world-building, magic systems, and more!

You can find more information on our website,
www.TCStudiosHQ.com.

#34 – "This was everything I had left." (F) (M) | (M) (G) (I)

Brainstorm (Writing) ...

- What have they lost?
    - How did they lose it?
    - Are they responsible?
        - Is someone else?
- What will they do now that they've lost it?
    - Will it be positive or negative?
- Will they try to get it back?
    - How might they do that?

Brainstorm (Drawing) ...

- What in their surroundings might give away what they've lost?
- Think about their expression when illustrating.
    - Do they look determined to get it back?
    - Do they look devastated that they've lost it?
    - Do they look like they're falling into madness?

Did you know?

We also publish novels and comics that you can read!

You can find more information on our website,
www.TCStudiosHQ.com.

#35 – "I can't believe they're gone." (M) (R) | (CP) (P) (W)

Brainstorm (Writing) …

- Who's gone?
    - What relation are they to this character?
- What happened to them?
    - Did they die?
    - Did they move?
    - What kind of context are they speaking in?
- What is happening or going to happen now that they're gone?
    - How are they coping, or how do they plan on coping?

Brainstorm (Drawing) …

- Think about how the meaning of this statement may influence the environment.
    - If the context is death, are they at a funeral?
        - Are they reminiscing?
    - If the context is relocation, are they missing them?

Do you want to give us a prompt for next year's edition?

You can submit prompt ideas you have based on next year's chapter themes. Credit will be given if selected.

You can find more information on our website, www.TCStudiosHQ.com.

#36 – "No …" (SF) (F) | (AP) (C) (I)

Brainstorm (Writing) …

- Are they answering a question?
- Are they in shock?
- Are they in denial?
- What is the story behind this statement?
    - What drove this character to say this so uncertainly?

Brainstorm (Drawing) …

- Think about the character's interaction.
    - Are they saying this to someone or something?
- Have they discovered something unpleasant?
    - Maybe they're having an unpleasant conversation.
- How could you position your character(s) to express the situation?

Drawing Exercise #4

Draw 10 different body languages that express sorrow.

#37 – "You're lying! They would never do that!" (D) (SL) | (P) (W) (G)

Brainstorm (Writing) …

- What has this third-party character been accused of?
  - Why is it so hard for this character to accept this accusation?
  - What does it say about either this character or the third-party character that the accusation is so unbelievable?
- What might the situation around the accusation be?
  - Is it illegal?
  - Is it intimate?

Brainstorm (Drawing) …

- Emotion!
  - Express the emotion of this yelling character.
  - How might the person being yelled at feel?
    - How might their body languages clash?
- Where is this scene playing out?
  - Could it change the way they're interacting?

Did you know?

We post daily writing & drawing prompts on our Social Medias for everyone to participate in.

Find us @PromptParty and use #PromptParty.

You can find more information on our website, www.TCStudiosHQ.com.

#38 – "I can't … Not without them …" (AA) (F) | (CP) (M) (I)

Brainstorm (Writing) …

- What are they being asked to do that they feel they can't?
  - Why do they think they can't?
- What is the basis for the request being asked of them?
  - Is it physical? Action-based?
  - Is it emotional?
- What will happen if they can't complete the task?

Brainstorm (Drawing) …

- Explore ways to express despair.
  - What might they look like with thoughts running through their head?
  - Have they been crying?
  - Do they look pale?

Did you know?

In addition to posting daily on Social Media, we have daily interactive posts on our YouTube channel, Podcast, and Blog.

You can find more information on our website, www.TCStudiosHQ.com.

#39 – "When will it end?" (D) (M) | (W) (C) (P)

Brainstorm (Writing) ...

- What is the tone of this question?
    - Is it said comically? With exaggeration?
    - Is it said in sorrow?
    - Is it said with impatience?
- When will *what* end?
    - How might the unknown factor change based on the tone of the question?

Brainstorm (Drawing) ...

- Draw the stage that provoked this question.
    - Think about the items and their placement in this person's surroundings that could influence the illustration.

Remember!

The listed genres/mediums and brainstorming boxes are **only suggestions!** We encourage you to do/use whatever you want.

45

#40 – "The tears just won't stop …" (F) (R) | (AP) (CP) (G)

Brainstorm (Writing) …

- What is happening to make this character cry?
    - How long have they been crying?
- Are they being forced to cry?
    - Are they under some kind of spell/curse?
        - Is it triggered by something?

Brainstorm (Drawing) …

- Maybe try exaggerating this scene.
    - Is the character sitting in a puddle of their own tears?
    - Are they holding a bucket full of them?
- Take an opportunity to practice drawing realistic tears/water.

You can share your work with us on Facebook, Instagram & Twitter!

Tag us @PromptParty and use #PromptParty.

We'd love to see what you come up with!

Chapter Five: Threatening.

#41 – "I dare you to say that again." (SL) (F) | (M) (CP) (W)

Brainstorm (Writing) ...

- What was said?
    - Why is this character so upset about it?
    - What are they going to do if it's said again?
- Does the person saying it care that it's been said?
    - Do they regret saying it?
    - Are they willing to defend their statement?

Brainstorm (Drawing) ...

- Picture this like a scene from an anime.
    - How can you dramatize the emotion in this character's eyes?
    - Consider your linework and the shading techniques you use.
    - Consider the positioning of the character's head and the lighting used on their face.

Writing Exercise #5

Write a scene where someone being threatened counters it successfully.

#42 – "You wanna bet?" (AA) | (C) (P) (G)

Brainstorm (Writing) ...

- What is being bet on?
  - Why are they confident enough to make a bet?
- What would the wager be?
  - Is it financial?
  - Is it an action?
  - Is it a favor?
- How might this relationship change because of the bet?
  - How might these characters feel if they know they're going to win or lose?
  - How might their behavior change?
  - Will they try to cheat?

Brainstorm (Drawing) ...

- Think about the confidence of the characters making a bet with each other.
  - How can you show that in their body language?
  - How can you show it in their expressions?

Do you want your work published?

You can submit any work made using our prompts to our annual anthologies! Published submissions receive shared 25% royalty.

You can find more information on our website,
www.TCStudiosHQ.com.

#43 – "Are you willing to risk your life for it?" (M) (AA) (H) | (G) (AP) (I)

Brainstorm (Writing) ...

- What is this character risking their life for?
    - Are they confident they can pull it off without dying?
    - Are they worried that they will die?
- Who is asking the question?
    - Is it someone on the sidelines, hearing about the task?
    - Is it the person providing the task?
        - Maybe a commander giving a spy a mission?
        - Maybe a chief fire fighter scoping out a dangerous job?

Brainstorm (Drawing) ...

- Think about how the context of this scenario could change your illustration.
    - If this is threatening, it may create a darker atmosphere.
    - If this is worrisome, it may create a grim atmosphere.

Did you know?

A percentage of every anthology sold goes towards helping communities like yours. This includes donations to charities, funding of scholarships, creating of programs, and more!

You can find more information on our website, www.TCStudiosHQ.com.

#44 – "You so much as speak her name again, and I'll kill you." (SL) (R) | (P) (M) (W)

Brainstorm (Writing) …

- Who is this character protecting?
    - o Their daughter? Their girlfriend?
- Who are they protecting her from?
    - o A crazy ex?
    - o A mobster?
- Think of how extreme this situation could be and the reason behind it.
    - o Is this character in the right? Or are they overreacting and acting out of line?
- Think of the perspective of all parties.
    - o Does she want to be protected?
    - o Is the third party dangerous? Are they determined?
        - ▪ Are they harmless and being discriminated against?

Brainstorm (Drawing) …

- Think about the tension that this threat carries.
- What are the different perspectives you can show?
    - o Is the person making the threat at their limit?
        - ▪ Do they look unhinged, or are they calm and matter of fact?
    - o Is the person being threatened scared, or are they confident and unphased?

Did you know?

In addition to our annual prompt anthologies, every year we have themed anthologies that you can also submit to!

You can find more information on our website, www.TCStudiosHQ.com.

#45 – "I wouldn't do that if I were you." (SF) (F) | (CP) (G) (I)

Brainstorm (Writing) ...

- What is the character being advised against?
  - Do they know that it's a bad idea?
  - Are they willing to do it anyway?
- Is the task actually dangerous?
  - If so, how?
  - If not, why is this character bluffing?
    - Is the bluff going to work?
      - What happens if it doesn't?
      - What happens if it does?

Brainstorm (Drawing) ...

- Play around with object use in your illustration.
  - Use this as an opportunity to practice drawing objects.
- What objects could be used in this scene?
  - How could the perspective of the objects emphasis what's happening in the scene?

Looking for a challenge?

Try doing one of our prompts with your friend(s)! See if you can come up with something together.

#46 – "Are you threatening me?" (SL) (AA) | (AP) (P) (C)

Brainstorm (Writing) …

- Who is being threatened?
    - And by whom?
        - What are they being threatened with?
        - Why?
- How does this character feel about being threatened?
    - Are they afraid?
    - Are they angry?
- What do they intend on doing about it?
    - Will they do what the aggressor says?
    - Will they retaliate?

Brainstorm (Drawing) …

- Pick a perspective to draw.
    - If you're drawing the aggressor, consider who they are and the position they're in the be making threats.
        - What location might this be taking place in?
    - If you're drawing the victim, consider their reaction.
        - How might anger or fear set up this frame?

Drawing Exercise #5

Draw a character with a threatening expression/body language.

#47 – "Do you even know who I am?" (AA) (D) | (C) (I) (W)

Brainstorm (Writing) …

- Who are they?
  - Why do they think they are able to be offended by the lack of acknowledgement?
- Where are they, and why would it matter if they're recognized?
- What's happening?
  - Why would they want to be able to use their identity in this situation?
    - Are they in a fight?
    - Are they being treated poorly by staff?
- What if this was asked in sorrow?
  - Could they be a forgotten lover?
  - Do their parents have dementia?
  - Are they the child of a parent that wasn't present?

Brainstorm (Drawing) …

- Focus on: Exaggeration.
  - If this is said in anger, how can you exaggerate this person's emotion?
    - Is their face red? Is there chest puffed? Is steam coming out of their ears?
  - If this is said in sorrow, how can you express the pain this person is feeling?
    - Are they crying? Are their brows pinched? Are they clutching at their heart?

Did you know?

We also make books to help with storytelling. With help on things like creating characters, world-building, magic systems, and more!

You can find more information on our website,
www.TCStudiosHQ.com.

#48 – "Just saying. That's a hell of a way to go." (H) (M) | (M) (P) (CP)

Brainstorm (Writing) …

- What form of death are they referring to?
    - Are they making a threat?
    - Are they genuinely advising them away?
- Who is taking the risk?
    - Why?
    - What would they get for risking their life?

Brainstorm (Drawing) …

- Show what this person is advising against in the layout and background of this illustration.
- Think about the body language of each party.
    - Express the warning/caution of the person advising.
    - Consider the expression of the person being advised.
        - Are they worried?
        - Are they defiant?

Did you know?

We also publish novels and comics that you can read!

You can find more information on our website,
www.TCStudiosHQ.com.

#49 – "Take your best shot." (F) (AA) | (C) (W) (P)

Brainstorm (Writing) ...

- What is this character being encouraged to do?
    - Throw a punch?
    - Throw a dart?
    - Fire a gun?
- How might what they're being encouraged to do effect the person encouraging them to do it?
    - What if it goes wrong?
    - What if it goes well?

Brainstorm (Drawing) ...

- Focus on: Environment.
    - Tell the story with the background or the characters' environment.
        - Maybe there's a dart board or a target in the distance.
        - Maybe the person speaking is pointing to their cheek with a very cocky grin.
            - Maybe there's a very rowdy crowd cheering them on.

Do you want to give us a prompt for next year's edition?

You can submit prompt ideas you have based on next year's chapter themes. Credit will be given if selected.

You can find more information on our website, www.TCStudiosHQ.com.

#50 – "I ain't scared of you." (AA) (SL) | (G) (AP) (I)

Brainstorm (Writing) ...

- Who is saying this statement, and to whom?
    - A kid to their bully?
    - An exterminator to a wasp hive?
- How are they about to prove that they aren't scared?
    - Do they need to prove it at all?
- What is the response of the person being told?

Brainstorm (Drawing) ...

- Play around with your shading techniques.
    - How can you emphasis the tension or the comic relief of the scene using shading and lighting?

Did you know?

We post daily writing & drawing prompts on our Social Medias for everyone to participate in.

Find us @PromptParty and use #PromptParty.

You can find more information on our website, www.TCStudiosHQ.com.

Chapter Six: Shock.

#51 – "What the hell?" (M) (F) | (I) (C) (CP)

Brainstorm (Writing) …

- How is this being said?
  - Fearfully?
  - Comically?
  - Dramatically?
- What is it being said in regards to, and how might the inflection affect the situation?

Brainstorm (Drawing) …

- Think about the facial expressions and how it can change the tone of the question.
- What about their surroundings? How might what's around them help tell the story?

Writing Exercise #6

Write a scene that ends with something unexpected.

#52 – "What are you doing?!" (SF) (M) | (W) (G) (AP)

Brainstorm (Writing) …

- Why is this person yelling?
    - Are they asking in horror?
    - Are they asking in rage?
- What might the reaction of the person being asked be?
    - Did they mean for this person do see them in action?
    - Are they glad they've been caught?
    - What are they going to do now?

Brainstorm (Drawing) …

- Challenge: Bird's Eye View.
    - Try drawing this piece with a bird's eye view.

Remember!

The listed genres/mediums and brainstorming boxes are **only suggestions!** We encourage you to do/use whatever you want.

#53 – "I … I can't believe this …" (M) (D) | (M) (P) (C)

Brainstorm (Writing) …

- What just happened?
  - o Have they lost a championship game?
  - o Have they just been betrayed?
  - o Have they just won the lottery?
- Play around with how you can spin this scenario.

Brainstorm (Drawing) …

- Experiment: Harsh Lighting.
  - o Experiment with using harsh lighting to color this piece. Use bold highlights and dark shadows.

You can share your work with us on Facebook, Instagram & Twitter!

Tag us @PromptParty and use #PromptParty.

We'd love to see what you come up with!

#54 – "You can't be serious." (SF) (AA) | (CP) (W) (G)

Brainstorm (Writing) …

- Why does this character think or hope someone is joking?
    - Could what they're talking about lead to injury or death?
    - Is it simply impractical?
    - Is it impossibly difficult to do?
    - Is it laughable?
- What is the person talking about and why?
    - Is there an end goal?
    - Is it personal?
- Think about the relationship between these characters and how this might affect it.

Brainstorm (Drawing) …

- Play around with effects. Think comics or manga.
    - Add effects around the character that emphasize how they're feeling.

Do you want your work published?

You can submit any work made using our prompts to our annual anthologies! Published submissions receive shared 25% royalties.

You can find more information on our website, www.TCStudiosHQ.com.

#55 – "It's headed straight for us!" (AA) (F) | (AP) (P) (I)

Brainstorm (Writing) …

- What is?
    - Is it an animal?
    - Is it a machine?
    - Is it a demon?
- What are these characters' reactions to it?
    - Do they fear it?
    - Are they happy about it?
- What are they going to do about it?
    - Run?
    - Stand their ground?

Brainstorm (Drawing) …

- Challenge: Opposite Colors.
    - Pick a color and its opposite (ex: red and green).
    - Try drawing this scene using only those two colors and their gradients.

Did you know?

A percentage of every anthology sold goes towards helping communities like yours. This includes donations to charities, funding of scholarships, creating of programs, and more!

You can find more information on our website, www.TCStudiosHQ.com.

#56 – "Ah!" (F) (R) | (C) (I) (W)

Brainstorm (Writing) …

- What just happened?
  - o Did they fall?
  - o Were they scared?
  - o Were they surprised?
  - o Did someone poke them?

Brainstorm (Drawing) …

- Consider what is causing the shock for this character – focus on illustrating the cause, rather than the reaction.

Drawing Exercise #6

Draw 10 expressions and/or body languages that express shock or surprise.

#57 – "Oh my god!" (H) (D) | (AP) (M) (CP)

Brainstorm (Writing) …

- How is this being said?
  - In fear?
  - In joy?
  - In disbelief?
  - In disgust?

Brainstorm (Drawing) …

- Challenge: No references.
  - Put your muscle memory to the test and draw this scene without using any references.
    - Good luck!

Did you know?

In addition to our annual prompt anthologies, every year we have <u>themed</u> anthologies that you can also submit to!

You can find more information on our website, www.TCStudiosHQ.com.

#58 – "No!" (H) (SF) (AA) | (P) (G) (AP)

Brainstorm (Writing) …

- How is this being said?
  - In dismay?
  - In anger?
- Why is this moment so intense?
- What's happening on the other side of the exclamation?

Brainstorm (Drawing) …

- Pick a facial feature to exaggerate as they yell.
  - Eyes.
  - Mouth.
  - Nose.
  - Eyebrows.

Looking for a challenge?

Try doing one of our prompts with your friend(s)! See if you can come up with something together.

#59 – "Don't! Don't do it!" (AA) (SF) | (I) (M) (P)

Brainstorm (Writing) …

- Think about the circumstances of the situation.
    - Who is talking?
    - Who are they talking to?
    - What are they trying to stop?
        - Do they actually have any power to stop it?
            - Maybe it's a comical reaction to a television show.
- Who's on the other side?
    - How do they feel about what's happening?
        - Do they care?
        - Do they want to do it?
        - What happens if they do?
        - What happens if they don't?

Brainstorm (Drawing) …

- Experiment: Comic Strip.
    - Try drawing this in two parts as a short comic strip.
        - A. "Don't!"
        - B. "Don't do it!"

Did you know?

We also make books to help with storytelling. With help on things like creating characters, world-building, magic systems, and more!

You can find more information on our website, www.TCStudiosHQ.com.

#60 – *Gasp* (M) | (AP) (CP) (W)

Brainstorm (Writing) …

- Why are they gasping?
    - Are they in pain?
    - Are they feeling pleasure?
    - Are they scared? Shocked?
- What happens after the gasp?
    - Are they angry?
    - Do they fight?

Brainstorm (Drawing) …

- Think of what the body does when it's in shock.
    - Think about how that changes depending on the type of shock.
        - i.e. smell, feeling, sight, etc.

Did you know?

We also publish novels and comics that you can read!

You can find more information on our website,
www.TCStudiosHQ.com.

Chapter Seven: Confused.

#61 – "I don't understand …" (SL) (M) (AA) | (G) (P) (CP)

Brainstorm (Writing) …

- Consider the emotional impact of whatever's just happened.
  - Write their state of mind without telling it.
  - Yes, they're confused, but what emotion is compounding that?
    - Anger?
    - Sorrow?
  - Write about how their emotions evolve from one to another, whichever it may be.

Brainstorm (Drawing) …

- Focus on: Environment.
  - How can you show what this character is confused about using the background, environment, and/or objects around them?

Writing Exercise #7

Write about a detective who is gathering conflicting information about an open case.

#62 – "Why are you doing this?" (SF) (R) (H) | (AP) (W) (I)

Brainstorm (Writing) ...

- Consider the gravity of what's happening.
    - What are they going to do about what's being done?
    - How will it affect their life and those around them?
        - Is there any way they can stop it?
            - How?
            - What happens if they can't?

- Challenge: Monochrome.
    - Try drawing this scene using only one gradient of color.

Do you want to give us a prompt for next year's edition?

You can submit prompt ideas you have based on next year's chapter themes. Credit will be given if selected.

You can find more information on our website, www.TCStudiosHQ.com.

#63 – "But this doesn't make any sense." (F) (SL) | (M) (C) (G)

Brainstorm (Writing) …

- What are they talking about?
  - A situation unfolding?
  - A map? A puzzle?
  - A government scheme?
- What needs to happen for them to understand?
  - What happens when they do?
  - What happens if they can't in time?
- Is there someone that's jumbling the situation on purpose?
  - What happens if they're found out?

Brainstorm (Drawing) …

- Practice different types of shading techniques.
  - Hatching.
  - Cross-Hatching.
  - Stippling.
  - Scribbling.
  - Contour Lines.

Did you know?

We post daily writing & drawing prompts on our Social Medias for everyone to participate in.

Find us @PromptParty and use #PromptParty.

You can find more information on our website, www.TCStudiosHQ.com.

#64 – "You can't just … Ugh!" (D) (AA) | (CP) (AP) (M)

Brainstorm (Writing) …

- What might be happening?
  - o Is someone giving up on words out of frustration?
  - o Were they interrupted with pain?
    - ▪ A wound? Were they punched?
- What's happening that they're upset about?
  - o Who's on the other end of it?
  - o How do they feel about what's happening?

Brainstorm (Drawing) …

- Experiment: Comic Strip.
  - o Try drawing this in two parts as a short comic strip.
    - ▪ A. "You can't just …"
    - ▪ B. "Ugh!"

Did you know?

In addition to posting daily on Social Media, we have daily interactive posts on our YouTube channel, Podcast, and Blog.

You can find more information on our website, www.TCStudiosHQ.com.

#65 – "Please, just tell me what's going on." (SF) (M) | (W) (P) (G)

Brainstorm (Writing) …

- What's the tone of this statement?
    - Is the person annoyed?
    - Are they desperate?
- What exactly is going on?
    - Has it been kept from this person on purpose?
    - What's going to happen when they find out?
    - Will they find out? Or will they be denied the information?

Brainstorm (Drawing) …

- Try drawing this with the focus being on the source of unknown information.
    - Maybe it's a group of gossiping people.
    - Maybe someone is being confronted about lying.

Remember!

The listed genres/mediums and brainstorming boxes are **only suggestions!** We encourage you to do/use whatever you want.

#66 – "Who are you? What do you want?" (F) (H) | (I) (C) (CP)

Brainstorm (Writing) ...

- Where are they that they don't know who they're speaking to?
  - Have they been kidnapped?
  - Do they have amnesia?
- Who are they talking to?
  - What do they want with them?
    - Are they trying to hurt them?
    - Do they want to help them?

Brainstorm (Drawing) ...

- Challenge: Primary Colors.
  - Try drawing this scene using only primary colors and their gradients.

Drawing Exercise #7

Draw something that creates two different images depending on how it's viewed.

72

#67 – "Where are we?" (AA) | (M) (AP) (G)

Brainstorm (Writing) ...

- Why don't they know where they are?
    - Were they blindfolded on the way there?
    - Were they knocked out?
        - Are they just now waking up?
- Who are they asking?
    - Someone they're trapped with?
    - The person that brought them there?

Brainstorm (Drawing) ...

- Have fun with your background!
    - Maybe draw a wild and mystical place full of wonders.

Remember!

The listed genres/mediums and brainstorming boxes are **only suggestions!** We encourage you to do/use whatever you want.

#68 – "Why can't I remember anything?" (M) (SF) | (P) (W) (CP)

Brainstorm (Writing) …

- Exercise:
  - Try writing a flashback that leads up to this question.
    - Be as detailed and include as many twists and turns as possible.

Brainstorm (Drawing) …

- What might the scene surrounding this question look like?
  - Is the character in a hospital?
    - Have they been drugged?
    - Do they have a bandage around their head?
  - Are they waking up in an unknown place?
    - An alien ship?
    - A prison cell?

You can share your work with us on Facebook, Instagram & Twitter!

Tag us @PromptParty and use #PromptParty.

We'd love to see what you come up with!

#69 – "You and your vocabulary … English, dammit!" (SL) | (I) (G) (C)

Brainstorm (Writing) …

- Craft a complex, hard to follow piece of dialogue, maybe something dealing with science or medicine.
    - Create an intense situation where the knowledge needs to be transferred, but the person getting it isn't capable of grasping the information.

Brainstorm (Drawing) …

- Exaggerate!
    - Get silly with this drawing.
        - Maybe exaggerate how annoyed this character is.
        - Maybe exaggerate how they're feeling with effects surrounding their character.
            - i.e. steam coming out of their ears or a symbol of frustration floating around their head.

Do you want your work published?

You can submit any work made using our prompts to our annual anthologies! Published submissions receive shared 25% royalties.

You can find more information on our website, www.TCStudiosHQ.com.

#70 – "What are you saying?" (R) (SF) | (AP) (M) (W)

Brainstorm (Writing) ...

- Why is the character confused?
    - Is someone speaking a different language?
    - Are they in denial?
- Is there any gravity behind what's being said?
    - Is there going to be a drastic change in this person's life because of it?

Brainstorm (Drawing) ...

- Emphasize this character's emotion with their facial and body language.
    - What are their hands doing?
    - How is their body positioned?
    - Where are they looking?
        - Are their eyes glazed over?

Did you know?

A percentage of every anthology sold goes towards helping communities like yours. This includes donations to charities, funding of scholarships, creating of programs, and more!

You can find more information on our website, www.TCStudiosHQ.com.

Chapter Eight: Hopeful.

#71 – "I can do this." (SL) (F) | (P) (M) (AP)

Brainstorm (Writing) ...

- Are they trying to psych themselves up?
    - o If yes, why are they feeling doubtful?
- Is this being said in confidence?
    - o What are they so confident about?
    - o How are they so confident?
- Are they trying to prove someone wrong?
    - o Who might that be?

Brainstorm (Drawing) ...

- Challenge: Bird's Eye View.
    - o Try drawing this piece with a bird's eye view.

Writing Exercise #8

Write a scene about characters in a seemingly hopeless situation –
then give them hope.

#72 – "It doesn't matter. We're going to make it through!" (SF) (AA) (F) | (G) (C) (W)

Brainstorm (Writing) ...

- Think about the intensity of the situation.
- What are they trying to get through?
  - An obstacle?
  - A personal situation?
- What happens if they fail?
  - Think about the consequences based on the type of obstacle they're trying to get through.

Brainstorm (Drawing) ...

- Consider the space that these characters are in.
  - Tell the story with what's around them.
    - Are they charging through a barrier?
    - Traveling through space and time?

Did you know?

In addition to our annual prompt anthologies, every year we have themed anthologies that you can also submit to!

You can find more information on our website, www.TCStudiosHQ.com.

#73 – "Go, go, go!" (AA) | (I) (CP) (P)

Brainstorm (Writing) ...

- Go where?
  - o Are they talking about getting from point A to point B?
  - o Are they riling themselves or someone else up?
- What is the emotion behind the exclamation?
  - o Are they determined?
  - o Are they worried?
  - o Are they angry?

Brainstorm (Drawing) ...

- Challenge: No references.
  - o Put your muscle memory to the test and draw this scene without using any references.
    - ▪ Good luck!

Looking for a challenge?

Try doing one of our prompts with your friend(s)! See if you can come up with something together.

#74 – "It finally stopped raining." (SL) (R) | (G) (M) (AP)

Brainstorm (Writing) …

- Where is this character?
  - Are they outside?
  - Are they inside looking out?
- Were they waiting for the rain to stop?
  - What are they waiting to do?

Brainstorm (Drawing) …

- What might their surroundings look like if it had been raining?
  - Play around with reflective puddles, wet surfaces, shining surfaces, etc.

Did you know?

We also make books to help with storytelling. With help on things like creating characters, world-building, magic systems, and more!

You can find more information on our website, www.TCStudiosHQ.com.

#75 – "Don't you dare give up." (F) (AA) | (W) (P) (I)

Brainstorm (Writing) …

- What are they struggling with?
  - Are they fighting death?
  - Are they working out?
  - Are they facing some kind of internal struggle?

Brainstorm (Drawing) …

- Maybe try drawing this character speaking to themselves in the mirror.
  - Use this as an excuse to practice drawing reverse images.

Did you know?

We also publish novels and comics that you can read!

You can find more information on our website, www.TCStudiosHQ.com.

#76 – "You've survived worse." (SL) (D) | (CP) (C) (AP)

Brainstorm (Writing) …

- Who is speaking?
    - Is someone telling this to this character?
    - Are they telling it to themselves?
- What have they been through?
    - What are they going through now?
    - What did they go through that it's being compared to?

Brainstorm (Drawing) …

- Try drawing this as a montage of memories.
- Try drawing this using the character's body to tell the story.
    - Do they have scars? Missing limbs?
    - What could you use to show the things this character has been through?

Drawing Exercise #8

Draw a collection of survival items.

82

#77 – "This is the moment we've been waiting for." (AA) (F) (SF) | (G) (M) (C)

Brainstorm (Writing) ...

- What has led to this moment?
    - What does this moment mean for these characters?
    - What happens when it's over?
- What happens if it doesn't go as planned?
    - What happens if it does?
    - Is anyone trying to stop this moment from happening?

Brainstorm (Drawing) ...

- Challenge: Monochrome.
    - Try drawing this scene using only one gradient of color.

You can share your work with us on Facebook, Instagram & Twitter!

Tag us @PromptParty and use #PromptParty.

We'd love to see what you come up with!

#78 – "Miracles really do exist." (D) (SF) | (M) (I) (P)

Brainstorm (Writing) ...

- What's happening to be called a miracle?
    - How do they feel about it?
    - How did they feel before this "miracle"?
- What had to happen to make this miracle exist?
    - Where sacrifices made?
        - What kind?
        - By whom?

Brainstorm (Drawing) ...

- Experiment: Back Lighting.
    - Try having your lighting placed behind your character(s).
    - How does this change the mood of the piece?

Do you want to give us a prompt for next year's edition?

You can submit prompt ideas you have based on next year's chapter themes. Credit will be given if selected.

You can find more information on our website, www.TCStudiosHQ.com.

#79 – "You're our last hope." (F) (AA) | (W) (CP) (C)

Brainstorm (Writing) …

- Who?
    - Who is speaking?
    - Who are they speaking to?
- Why?
    - Why are they their last hope?
- What?
    - What do they have to do?
- How?
    - How do they feel about having so much pressure on them?
        - Do they accept the responsibility?
    - How are they going to get things done?

Brainstorm (Drawing) …

- Challenge: Self-Portrait.
    - Draw yourself into this scene.
    - Are you the one asking for help, or this person's savior?

Did you know?

We post daily writing & drawing prompts on our Social Medias for everyone to participate in.

Find us @PromptParty and use #PromptParty.

You can find more information on our website, www.TCStudiosHQ.com.

#80 – "Almost … there …" (SL) (F) (SF) | (AP) (I) (G)

Brainstorm (Writing) …

- What are they in the process of doing?
  - Completing a project?
  - Climbing a mountain?
- What happens when it's achieved?
- What happens if it's not?
- Who is involved in the process?
  - How do they feel about it?
  - What are their roles?

Brainstorm (Drawing) …

- Experiment: Exaggerated Proportions/Features.
  - Get a little cartoony.
  - How might exaggerating certain features relate to the story behind the image?

Did you know?

In addition to posting daily on Social Media, we have daily interactive posts on our YouTube channel, Podcast, and Blog.

You can find more information on our website, www.TCStudiosHQ.com.

Chapter Nine: Desperate.

#81 – "Please …" (R) (H) | (C) (I) (AP)

Brainstorm (Writing) …

- Why are they begging?
    - Are they asking someone, or praying?
- Are they begging at all?
    - Are they saying this in jest?
    - Are they cocky? Talking down to someone?
- Does it matter?
    - Consider the other half of the conversation.
    - What are they doing?
        - Are they phased by the begging?

Brainstorm (Drawing) …

- Challenge: Color Palette.
    - Use a random color palette generator or ask a friend to pick 5 colors for you to use.

Writing Exercise #9

Write a scene of someone acting out of desperation.

#82 – "I'll do anything." (SL) | (CP) (W) (P)

Brainstorm (Writing) …

- What's putting them in a position to say this?
  - Are they being threatened?
    - With what?
- What are they willing to do?
  - What do they have the means to do?

Brainstorm (Drawing) …

- Try drawing what will happen if this character doesn't follow through with their claim.
  - Maybe someone is threatening them with an image, or legal notice.

Remember!

The listed genres/mediums and brainstorming boxes are **only suggestions!** We encourage you to do/use whatever you want.

#83 – "This is the only way I can see him again." (D) (R) | (I) (M) (G)

Brainstorm (Writing) ...

- Who are they talking about?
    - A friend? A mentor?
    - A child? A lover?
- What is it that they have to do?
    - Is it financial?
    - Is it physical?
    - What will it cost them?
        - Physically?
        - Mentally?
        - Emotionally?
        - Financially?

Brainstorm (Drawing) ...

- Think about how distraught this person must be, how desperate they've become.
    - Think about how that translates to their expression, appearance, and surroundings.

You can share your work with us on Facebook, Instagram & Twitter!

Tag us @PromptParty and use #PromptParty.

We'd love to see what you come up with!

#84 – "Just a little. I swear I won't tell anyone." (SL) (SF) | (I) (W) (M)

Brainstorm (Writing) …

- What are they being secretive about?
  - Why must it be a secret?
  - What are they getting?
- How does this character feel?
  - Are they desperate for something?
  - Are they trying to bribe someone?

Brainstorm (Drawing) …

- Challenge: Continuous line.
  - Tray drawing this scene with one continuous line.
  - You can color the finished image.

Do you want your work published?

You can submit any work made using our prompts to our annual anthologies! Published submissions receive shared 25% royalties.

You can find more information on our website,
www.TCStudiosHQ.com.

#85 – "Just tell me what you want!" (R) (F) | (AP) (CP) (G)

Brainstorm (Writing) …

- Who are they talking to?
    - A husband to his partner?
    - Their God?
    - A demon?
- What has them so worked up?
- What if they can't figure it out?

Brainstorm (Drawing) …

- Consider this character's emotion.
    - Are they red in the face from anger?
    - Are they red in the face from sobbing?

Did you know?

A percentage of every anthology sold goes towards helping communities like yours. This includes donations to charities, funding of scholarships, creating of programs, and more!

You can find more information on our website, www.TCStudiosHQ.com.

#86 – "I don't have a choice." (AA) (M) | (C) (P) (I)

Brainstorm (Writing) …

- What are they being forced to do?
    - What does that mean for them?
        - What does it mean for their loved ones?
- Who are they telling?
    - Does this person want to stop them?
    - Are they willing to help them?

Brainstorm (Drawing) …

- Draw this character in the process of what they're about to do.
    - Think about what their body placement might be like.
        - Is it on edge? Nervous?
        - Do they seem rigid?

Drawing Exercise #9

Draw a short comic strip of someone in a desperate situation.

#87 – "Whatever it takes." (D) (F) (SF) | (M) (W) (AP)

Brainstorm (Writing) …

- Why is this character so determined?
    - What have they been through?
    - What are they about to go through?
        - What are they going to get out of it?
- What are they willing to do?
    - Are they going to have any help?
    - Are they going to put themselves in danger?
- What is the goal?
    - To save someone? To save themselves?
    - To defeat an enemy?
    - To accomplish a dream?

Brainstorm (Drawing) …

- Experiment: Bold Line Work.
    - When you've finished lining your work (if you're lining), try making some areas thicker than others.
        - It can be dramatically, or just a bit.
            - Take note of how it changes the tone of your work.

Did you know?

In addition to our annual prompt anthologies, every year we have themed anthologies that you can also submit to!

You can find more information on our website, www.TCStudiosHQ.com.

#88 – "Just talk to me …" (R) (SL) | (G) (CP) (C)

Brainstorm (Writing) …

- Who are they asking to speak?
    - Why won't they speak to them?
    - What will it take to get them to talk?
    - What are they hoping to have resolved?

Brainstorm (Drawing) …

- Think about the positioning of these characters.
    - Is the begging person clinging to the other?
    - Are they keeping their distance with caution?
    - What about the second party?
        - Are they reluctant to engage?
        - Are they a nervous wreck?
        - Is something preventing them from speaking?

Looking for a challenge?

Try doing one of our prompts with your friend(s)! See if you can come up with something together.

#89 – "You don't have to do this." (H) (AA) | (P) (I) (M)

Brainstorm (Writing) …

- What don't they have to do?
    - Is it true, or is this character just trying to keep them out of danger?
    - If it's true, what could be done instead?
- Why is this character willing to do it?
    - What will it mean if they do?
    - What will it mean if they don't?

Brainstorm (Drawing) …

- Focus on: Background.
    - Tell the story with the use of the background and its environment. Think about the use and placement of specific items to help get the point across.

Did you know?

We also make books to help with storytelling. With help on things like creating characters, world-building, magic systems, and more!

You can find more information on our website, www.TCStudiosHQ.com.

#90 – "Take me instead." (D) (H) | (W) (G) (AP)

Brainstorm (Writing) …

- Who are they talking to?
    - A mobster?
    - God?
    - The Grim Reaper?
- Who are they asking to be replaced?
    - Their child?
    - Their lover?
    - Their friend?
- What would being taken mean for either of them?
    - Death?
    - Enslavement?
    - Paradise?

Brainstorm (Drawing) …

- Think about the possible context options above.
    - How might they change the expressions and surroundings of this scene?

Did you know?

We also publish novels and comics that you can read!

You can find more information on our website,
www.TCStudiosHQ.com.

Chapter Ten: Betrayal.

#91 – "You weren't supposed to see this." (R) (M) (H) | (G) (I) (P)

Brainstorm (Writing) …

- What just happened?
    - Murder?
    - An affair?
    - A surprise present/party?
- What's going to happen now that it's been seen?

Brainstorm (Drawing) …

- Pick a perspective to draw.
    - Either the offended or the offender.
- What might either of their expressions tell about what's just happened?
    - Maybe play around with the reflection in either of their eyes.

Writing Exercise #10

Write a scene of someone summarizing their betrayal – then plotting their revenge.

#92 – "… Babe?" (R) | (C) (AP) (W)

Brainstorm (Writing) …

- Why are they so hesitant to call out?
    - Did they just witness something?
    - Is something happening to them?
- What in their tone of voice?
    - Are they in physical pain?
    - Are they feeling nervous? Scared?
    - Are they in shock? Denial?

Brainstorm (Drawing) …

- Challenge: No Linework.
    - Tray drawing this scene with no outlining – just dive right in with blocks of color!

Do you want to give us a prompt for next year's edition?

You can submit prompt ideas you have based on next year's chapter themes. Credit will be given if selected.

You can find more information on our website, www.TCStudiosHQ.com.

#93 – "…by my own brother …" (SL) (F) | (M) (CP) (I)

Brainstorm (Writing) …

- What did the brother do?
    - Stab them?
    - Betray them?
        - How so?
- What do they intend on doing about it?
    - Is there anything that can be done?
    - How would they go about doing it?
- Consider the perspective of the brother.
    - How do they feel about what's happening?
    - Why are they doing it?
    - What's next for them?

Brainstorm (Drawing) …

- Try to depict the gravity of the situation through each character's body language (if you are drawing both characters).
    - Are their shoulders slumped?
    - Have they fallen on their knees?
    - Is their face in their hands?

Did you know?

We post daily writing & drawing prompts on our Social Medias for everyone to participate in.

Find us @PromptParty and use #PromptParty.

You can find more information on our website, www.TCStudiosHQ.com.

#94 – "I'm not asking you to forgive me." (SF) (M) | (P) (AP) (G)

Brainstorm (Writing) …

- What have they done?
    - Why don't they feel the need to be sorry?
- Who have they done it to?
    - Was it intentional?

Brainstorm (Drawing) …

- Think about the emotion of the person saying this.
    - How might their facial expression change the context of what's going on?
        - Are they angry?
        - Are they sorry?

Did you know?

In addition to posting daily on Social Media, we have daily interactive posts on our YouTube channel, Podcast, and Blog.

You can find more information on our website, www.TCStudiosHQ.com.

#95 – "It was the only way." (D) (F) (SF) | (C) (CP) (W)

Brainstorm (Writing) …

- What has this character done?
  - ○ Was it drastic?
  - ○ Was it deadly?
  - ○ Was it foolish?
- Who are they explaining it to?
  - ○ How does this action affect them?
  - ○ How do they feel about what this character's done?
  - ○ Are they happy with the outcome?

Brainstorm (Drawing) …

- Think about the aftermath of this situation.
  - ○ Is this person covered in blood?
  - ○ Are they wounded?
  - ○ Are they holding something that might give a bit of context?
  - ○ Tell as much story with the image as you can.

Remember!

The listed genres/mediums and brainstorming boxes are **only suggestions!** We encourage you to do/use whatever you want.

#96 – "There's someone else." (R) (H) | (I) (M) (G)

Brainstorm (Writing) …

- Think about the possible context.
    - Are they talking about a lover?
    - Are they talking about a business partner?
    - Are they talking about a loose end?
- How is this being said?
    - With despair?
    - With relief?
    - With caution?

Brainstorm (Drawing) …

- Experiment: Colored Lighting.
    - When/if you are applying lighting effects to this piece, try using a different color instead of just a lighter gradient of the lit area.

Drawing Exercise #10

Tell a story of betrayal with your illustration.

102

#97 – "Is it sinking in, yet?" (M) (AA) | (P) (AP) (C)

Brainstorm (Writing) …

- What's going on?
    - ○ Is someone being betrayed?
    - ○ Is someone making a threat?
    - ○ Is this a literal statement?
- If it's not literal, consider both perspectives.
    - ○ What position is either party in?
    - ○ How do they feel about whatever's being done?

Brainstorm (Drawing) …

- Challenge: Monochrome.
    - ○ Try drawing this scene using only one gradient of color.

You can share your work with us on Facebook, Instagram & Twitter!

Tag us @PromptParty and use #PromptParty.

We'd love to see what you come up with!

#98 – "You were a tool. Nothing more." (F) (R) (AA) | (W) (CP) (I)

Brainstorm (Writing) ...

- What relationship is surrounding these characters?
    - Are/were they in a romantic relationship?
    - Are/were they teacher and student?
    - Are/were they commander and soldier?
- Play around with how the situation could change based on the relationship these characters have.

Brainstorm (Drawing) ...

- Play around with perspective and foreshadowing.
    - Maybe there's a fisheye view of the reaction of the person they are telling.
    - Maybe they're standing at a distance with an exaggerated shadow.
- Try to capture the gravity of the situation using perspective and foreshadowing.

Do you want your work published?

You can submit any work made using our prompts to our annual anthologies! Published submissions receive shared 25% royalties.

You can find more information on our website, www.TCStudiosHQ.com.

#99 – "I can't believe you'd do this to me." (SL) | (G) (P) (M)

Brainstorm (Writing) …

- What's been done that's so offensive?
    - What happened in these characters' pasts that would make this so intense?
- What is this character going to do in response?
    - Has this event broken them?
    - Do they want revenge?
    - Are they willing to forgive them?

Brainstorm (Drawing) …

- Think about drawing this from the perspective of the offender.
    - Draw them in the process, or in the wake of what they've done to this character.
    - Try to capture how they feel about it in their facial and body language.
        - Are they regretful?
        - Are they content?
        - Are they disinterested?

Did you know?

A percentage of every anthology sold goes towards helping communities like yours. This includes donations to charities, funding of scholarships, creating of programs, and more!

You can find more information on our website, www.TCStudiosHQ.com.

#100 – "Just tell me the truth!" (R) (M) | (C) (AP) (I)

Brainstorm (Writing) …

- Has someone been lying?
    - If they are – what about?
    - If they aren't – what are they being accused of?
- How long has the supposed lie been going on?
    - Is it new, and this person has just reached their limit?
- What will they do with the truth?
    - Will they be able to handle it?

Brainstorm (Drawing) …

- Focus on: Hands.
    - What are their hands doing?
        - Shaking?
        - Clenched into fists?
        - Begging?
    - Think about how the language of their hands may relate to the language of their facial expression.

Be The First To Know.

Join our newsletter and be the first to know about new prompt books, novels, comics, giveaways, freebies, coupons, and anything else we've got going on!

Find our newsletter on our website, www.TCStudiosHQ.com.

Prompts By Genre

Fantasy (F)

1. #2 – "What are those things?!"
2. #14 – "How dare you."
3. #33 – "We can't just let them die out there."
4. #34 – "This was everything I had left."
5. #36 – "No …"
6. #38 – "I can't … Not without them …"
7. #40 – "The tears just won't stop …"
8. #41 – "I dare you to say that again."
9. #45 – "I wouldn't do that if I were you."
10. #49 – "Take your best shot."
11. #51 – "What the hell?"
12. #55 – "It's headed straight for us!"
13. #56 – "Ah!"
14. #63 – "But this doesn't make any sense."
15. #66 – "Who are you? What do you want?"
16. #71 – "I can do this."
17. #72 – "It doesn't matter. We're going to make it through!"
18. #75 – "Don't you dare give up."
19. #77 – "This is the moment we've been waiting for."
20. #79 – "You're our last hope."
21. #80 – "Almost … there …"
22. #85 – "Just tell me what you want!"
23. #87 – "Whatever it takes."
24. #93 – "…by my own brother …"
25. #95 – "It was the only way."
26. #98 – "You were a tool. Nothing more."

Science Fiction (SF)

1. #6 – "Are they dead?"
2. #17 – "You're a monster!"
3. #20 – "What the hell's going on here?!"
4. #29 – "There's nothing I wouldn't do for my child."

5. #31 – "Please … Make it stop."
6. #36 – "No …"
7. #45 – "I wouldn't do that if I were you."
8. #52 – "What are you doing?!"
9. #54 – "You can't be serious."
10. #58 – "No!"
11. #59 – "Don't! Don't do it!"
12. #62 – "Why are you doing this?"
13. #65 – "Please, just tell me what's going on."
14. #68 – "Why can't I remember anything?"
15. #70 – "What are you saying?"
16. #72 – "It doesn't matter. We're going to make it through!"
17. #77 – "This is the moment we've been waiting for."
18. #78 – "Miracles really do exist."
19. #80 – "Almost … there …"
20. #84 – "Just a little. I swear I won't tell anyone."
21. #87 – "Whatever it takes."
22. #94 – "I'm not asking you to forgive me."
23. #95 – "It was the only way."

Romance (R)

1. #5 – "What have I done?"
2. #16 – "You're nothing but a liar!"
3. #21 – "You're everything I've ever wanted."
4. #22 – "Please come home."
5. #24 – "I'll always be there for you."
6. #26 – "I love you."
7. #28 – "This isn't love!"
8. #30 – "They … told me they loved me."
9. #35 – "I can't believe they're gone."
10. #40 – "The tears just won't stop …"
11. #44 – "You so much as speak her name again, and I'll kill you."
12. #56 – "Ah!"
13. #62 – "Why are you doing this?"
14. #70 – "What are you saying?"
15. #74 – "It finally stopped raining."
16. #81 – "Please …"
17. #83 – "This is the only way I can see him again."

18. #85 – "Just tell me what you want!"
19. #88 – "Just talk to me …"
20. #91 – "You weren't supposed to see this."
21. #92 – "… Babe?"
22. #96 – "There's someone else."
23. #98 – "You were a tool. Nothing more."
24. #100 – "Just tell me the truth!"

Horror (H)

1. #1 – "Did you hear that?"
2. #2 – "What are those things?!"
3. #3 – "They're … They're coming for us."
4. #4 – "Please …No … No!"
5. #6 – "Are they dead?"
6. #8 – "There's someone in the house."
7. #9 – "We're not alone."
8. #12 – "I'll kill you!"
9. #25 – "I'm sure they're watching over us."
10. #43 – "Are you willing to risk your life for it?"
11. #48 – "Just saying. That's a hell of a way to go."
12. #57 – "Oh my god!"
13. #58 – "No!"
14. #62 – "Why are you doing this?"
15. #66 – "Who are you? What do you want?"
16. #81 – "Please …"
17. #89 – "You don't have to do this."
18. #90 – "Take me instead."
19. #91 – "You weren't supposed to see this."
20. #96 – "There's someone else."

Dystopian (D)

1. #3 – "They're … They're coming for us."
2. #18 – "We can't just sit here and do nothing."
3. #22 – "Please come home."
4. #28 – "This isn't love!"
5. #31 – "Please … Make it stop."
6. #32 – "How can they do this to us?"

7. #37 – "You're lying! They would never do that!"
8. #39 – "When will it end?"
9. #47 – "Do you even know who I am?"
10. #53 – "I … I can't believe this …"
11. #57 – "Oh my god!"
12. #64 – "You can't just … Ugh!"
13. #76 – "You've survived worse."
14. #78 – "Miracles really do exist."
15. #83 – "This is the only way I can see him again."
16. #87 – "Whatever it takes."
17. #90 – "Take me instead."
18. #95 – "It was the only way."

Slice Of Life (SL)

1. #4 – "Please …No … No!"
2. #5 – "What have I done?"
3. #7 – "What am I supposed to do, now?!"
4. #10 – "Get it off, get it off!"
5. #11 – "Don't you dare."
6. #13 – "You've got some nerve."
7. #14 – "How dare you."
8. #15 – "Fuck off!"
9. #16 – "You're nothing but a liar!"
10. #19 – "Just who do you think you are?"
11. #20 – "What the hell's going on here?!"
12. #23 – "Everyone makes sacrifices."
13. #25 – "I'm sure they're watching over us."
14. #27 – "It's my passion."
15. #29 – "There's nothing I wouldn't do for my child."
16. #30 – "They … told me they loved me."
17. #37 – "You're lying! They would never do that!"
18. #41 – "I dare you to say that again."
19. #44 – "You so much as speak her name again, and I'll kill you."
20. #46 – "Are you threatening me?"
21. #50 – "I ain't scared of you."
22. #61 – "I don't understand …"
23. #63 – "But this doesn't make any sense."
24. #69 – "You and your vocabulary … English, dammit!"

25. #71 – "I can do this."
26. #74 – "It finally stopped raining."
27. #76 – "You've survived worse."
28. #80 – "Almost … there …"
29. #82 – "I'll do anything."
30. #84 – "Just a little. I swear I won't tell anyone."
31. #88 – "Just talk to me …"
32. #93 – "…by my own brother …"
33. #99 – "I can't believe you'd do this to me."

Action & Adventure (AA)

1. #3 – "They're … They're coming for us."
2. #7 – "What am I supposed to do, now?!"
3. #12 – "I'll kill you!"
4. #15 – "Fuck off!"
5. #18 – "We can't just sit here and do nothing."
6. #23 – "Everyone makes sacrifices."
7. #29 – "There's nothing I wouldn't do for my child."
8. #32 – "How can they do this to us?"
9. #33 – "We can't just let them die out there."
10. #38 – "I can't … Not without them …"
11. #42 – "You wanna bet?"
12. #43 – "Are you willing to risk your life for it?"
13. #46 – "Are you threatening me?"
14. #47 – "Do you even know who I am?"
15. #49 – "Take your best shot."
16. #50 – "I ain't scared of you."
17. #54 – "You can't be serious."
18. #55 – "It's headed straight for us!"
19. #58 – "No!"
20. #59 – "Don't! Don't do it!"
21. #61 – "I don't understand …"
22. #64 – "You can't just … Ugh!"
23. #67 – "Where are we?"
24. #72 – "It doesn't matter. We're going to make it through!"
25. #73 – "Go, go, go!"
26. #75 – "Don't you dare give up."
27. #77 – "This is the moment we've been waiting for."

28. #79 – "You're our last hope."
29. #86 – "I don't have a choice."
30. #89 – "You don't have to do this."
31. #97 – "Is it sinking in, yet?"
32. #98 – "You were a tool. Nothing more."

Mystery (M)

1. #8 – "There's someone in the house."
2. #19 – "Just who do you think you are?"
3. #20 – "What the hell's going on here?!"
4. #34 – "This was everything I had left."
5. #35 – "I can't believe they're gone."
6. #39 – "When will it end?"
7. #43 – "Are you willing to risk your life for it?"
8. #48 – "Just saying. That's a hell of a way to go."
9. #51 – "What the hell?"
10. #52 – "What are you doing?!"
11. #53 – "I … I can't believe this …"
12. #60 – *Gasp*
13. #61 – "I don't understand …"
14. #65 – "Please, just tell me what's going on."
15. #68 – "Why can't I remember anything?"
16. #86 – "I don't have a choice."
17. #91 – "You weren't supposed to see this."
18. #94 – "I'm not asking you to forgive me."
19. #97 – "Is it sinking in, yet?"
20. #100 – "Just tell me the truth!"

Prompts By Medium

Pencil (P)

1. #2 – "What are those things?!"
2. #4 – "Please …No … No!"
3. #7 – "What am I supposed to do, now?!"
4. #10 – "Get it off, get it off!"
5. #11 – "Don't you dare."
6. #14 – "How dare you."
7. #16 – "You're nothing but a liar!"
8. #20 – "What the hell's going on here?!"
9. #23 – "Everyone makes sacrifices."
10. #26 – "I love you."
11. #29 – "There's nothing I wouldn't do for my child."
12. #30 – "They … told me they loved me."
13. #33 – "We can't just let them die out there."
14. #35 – "I can't believe they're gone."
15. #37 – "You're lying! They would never do that!"
16. #39 – "When will it end?"
17. #42 – "You wanna bet?"
18. #44 – "You so much as speak her name again, and I'll kill you."
19. #46 – "Are you threatening me?"
20. #48 – "Just saying. That's a hell of a way to go."
21. #49 – "Take your best shot."
22. #53 – "I … I can't believe this …"
23. #55 – "It's headed straight for us!"
24. #58 – "No!"
25. #59 – "Don't! Don't do it!"
26. #61 – "I don't understand …"
27. #65 – "Please, just tell me what's going on."
28. #68 – "Why can't I remember anything?"
29. #71 – "I can do this."
30. #73 – "Go, go, go!"
31. #75 – "Don't you dare give up."
32. #78 – "Miracles really do exist."
33. #82 – "I'll do anything."

34. #86 – "I don't have a choice."
35. #89 – "You don't have to do this."
36. #91 – "You weren't supposed to see this."
37. #94 – "I'm not asking you to forgive me."
38. #97 – "Is it sinking in, yet?"
39. #99 – "I can't believe you'd do this to me."

Marker (M)

1. #1 – "Did you hear that?"
2. #3 – "They're … They're coming for us."
3. #7 – "What am I supposed to do, now?!"
4. #9 – "We're not alone."
5. #13 – "You've got some nerve."
6. #15 – "Fuck off!"
7. #17 – "You're a monster!"
8. #19 – "Just who do you think you are?"
9. #21 – "You're everything I've ever wanted."
10. #24 – "I'll always be there for you."
11. #26 – "I love you."
12. #29 – "There's nothing I wouldn't do for my child."
13. #32 – "How can they do this to us?"
14. #34 – "This was everything I had left."
15. #38 – "I can't … Not without them …"
16. #41 – "I dare you to say that again."
17. #44 – "You so much as speak her name again, and I'll kill you."
18. #48 – "Just saying. That's a hell of a way to go."
19. #53 – "I … I can't believe this …"
20. #57 – "Oh my god!"
21. #59 – "Don't! Don't do it!"
22. #63 – "But this doesn't make any sense."
23. #64 – "You can't just … Ugh!"
24. #67 – "Where are we?"
25. #70 – "What are you saying?"
26. #71 – "I can do this."
27. #74 – "It finally stopped raining."
28. #77 – "This is the moment we've been waiting for."
29. #78 – "Miracles really do exist."
30. #83 – "This is the only way I can see him again."

116

31. #84 – "Just a little. I swear I won't tell anyone."
32. #87 – "Whatever it takes."
33. #89 – "You don't have to do this."
34. #93 – "…by my own brother …"
35. #96 – "There's someone else."
36. #99 – "I can't believe you'd do this to me."

Ink (I)

1. #1 – "Did you hear that?"
2. #4 – "Please …No … No!"
3. #6 – "Are they dead?"
4. #9 – "We're not alone."
5. #11 – "Don't you dare."
6. #14 – "How dare you."
7. #17 – "You're a monster!"
8. #19 – "Just who do you think you are?"
9. #22 – "Please come home."
10. #26 – "I love you."
11. #28 – "This isn't love!"
12. #30 – "They … told me they loved me."
13. #31 – "Please … Make it stop."
14. #33 – "We can't just let them die out there."
15. #34 – "This was everything I had left."
16. #36 – "No …"
17. #38 – "I can't … Not without them …"
18. #43 – "Are you willing to risk your life for it?"
19. #45 – "I wouldn't do that if I were you."
20. #47 – "Do you even know who I am?"
21. #50 – "I ain't scared of you."
22. #51 – "What the hell?"
23. #55 – "It's headed straight for us!"
24. #56 – "Ah!"
25. #59 – "Don't! Don't do it!"
26. #62 – "Why are you doing this?"
27. #66 – "Who are you? What do you want?"
28. #69 – "You and your vocabulary … English, dammit!"
29. #73 – "Go, go, go!"
30. #75 – "Don't you dare give up."

31. #78 – "Miracles really do exist."
32. #80 – "Almost … there …"
33. #81 – "Please …"
34. #83 – "This is the only way I can see him again."
35. #84 – "Just a little. I swear I won't tell anyone."
36. #86 – "I don't have a choice."
37. #89 – "You don't have to do this."
38. #91 – "You weren't supposed to see this."
39. #93 – "…by my own brother …"
40. #96 – "There's someone else."
41. #98 – "You were a tool. Nothing more."
42. #100 – "Just tell me the truth!"

Crayon (C)

1. #3 – "They're … They're coming for us."
2. #5 – "What have I done?"
3. #6 – "Are they dead?"
4. #9 – "We're not alone."
5. #12 – "I'll kill you!"
6. #15 – "Fuck off!"
7. #18 – "We can't just sit here and do nothing."
8. #23 – "Everyone makes sacrifices."
9. #25 – "I'm sure they're watching over us."
10. #27 – "It's my passion."
11. #32 – "How can they do this to us?"
12. #36 – "No …"
13. #39 – "When will it end?"
14. #42 – "You wanna bet?"
15. #46 – "Are you threatening me?"
16. #47 – "Do you even know who I am?"
17. #49 – "Take your best shot."
18. #51 – "What the hell?"
19. #53 – "I … I can't believe this …"
20. #56 – "Ah!"
21. #63 – "But this doesn't make any sense."
22. #66 – "Who are you? What do you want?"
23. #69 – "You and your vocabulary … English, dammit!"
24. #72 – "It doesn't matter. We're going to make it through!"

25. #76 – "You've survived worse."
26. #77 – "This is the moment we've been waiting for."
27. #79 – "You're our last hope."
28. #81 – "Please …"
29. #86 – "I don't have a choice."
30. #88 – "Just talk to me …"
31. #92 – "… Babe?"
32. #95 – "It was the only way."
33. #97 – "Is it sinking in, yet?"
34. #100 – "Just tell me the truth!"

Gouache (G)

1. #2 – "What are those things?!"
2. #5 – "What have I done?"
3. #8 – "There's someone in the house."
4. #10 – "Get it off, get it off!"
5. #11 – "Don't you dare."
6. #13 – "You've got some nerve."
7. #18 – "We can't just sit here and do nothing."
8. #22 – "Please come home."
9. #24 – "I'll always be there for you."
10. #27 – "It's my passion."
11. #30 – "They … told me they loved me."
12. #31 – "Please … Make it stop."
13. #34 – "This was everything I had left."
14. #37 – "You're lying! They would never do that!"
15. #40 – "The tears just won't stop …"
16. #42 – "You wanna bet?"
17. #43 – "Are you willing to risk your life for it?"
18. #45 – "I wouldn't do that if I were you."
19. #50 – "I ain't scared of you."
20. #52 – "What are you doing?!"
21. #54 – "You can't be serious."
22. #58 – "No!"
23. #61 – "I don't understand …"
24. #63 – "But this doesn't make any sense."
25. #65 – "Please, just tell me what's going on."
26. #67 – "Where are we?"

27. #69 – "You and your vocabulary … English, dammit!"
28. #72 – "It doesn't matter. We're going to make it through!"
29. #74 – "It finally stopped raining."
30. #77 – "This is the moment we've been waiting for."
31. #80 – "Almost … there …"
32. #83 – "This is the only way I can see him again."
33. #85 – "Just tell me what you want!"
34. #88 – "Just talk to me …"
35. #90 – "Take me instead."
36. #91 – "You weren't supposed to see this."
37. #94 – "I'm not asking you to forgive me."
38. #96 – "There's someone else."
39. #99 – "I can't believe you'd do this to me."

Acrylic Paint (AP)

1. #2 – "What are those things?!"
2. #6 – "Are they dead?"
3. #8 – "There's someone in the house."
4. #13 – "You've got some nerve."
5. #16 – "You're nothing but a liar!"
6. #19 – "Just who do you think you are?"
7. #21 – "You're everything I've ever wanted."
8. #23 – "Everyone makes sacrifices."
9. #25 – "I'm sure they're watching over us."
10. #28 – "This isn't love!"
11. #31 – "Please … Make it stop."
12. #36 – "No …"
13. #40 – "The tears just won't stop …"
14. #43 – "Are you willing to risk your life for it?"
15. #46 – "Are you threatening me?"
16. #50 – "I ain't scared of you."
17. #52 – "What are you doing?!"
18. #55 – "It's headed straight for us!"
19. #57 – "Oh my god!"
20. #58 – "No!"
21. #60 – *Gasp*
22. #62 – "Why are you doing this?"
23. #64 – "You can't just … Ugh!"

24. #67 – "Where are we?"
25. #70 – "What are you saying?"
26. #71 – "I can do this."
27. #74 – "It finally stopped raining."
28. #76 – "You've survived worse."
29. #80 – "Almost … there …"
30. #81 – "Please …"
31. #85 – "Just tell me what you want!"
32. #87 – "Whatever it takes."
33. #90 – "Take me instead."
34. #92 – "… Babe?"
35. #94 – "I'm not asking you to forgive me."
36. #97 – "Is it sinking in, yet?"
37. #100 – "Just tell me the truth!"

Color Pencil (CP)

1. #1 – "Did you hear that?"
2. #4 – "Please …No … No!"
3. #7 – "What am I supposed to do, now?!"
4. #12 – "I'll kill you!"
5. #15 – "Fuck off!"
6. #17 – "You're a monster!"
7. #20 – "What the hell's going on here?!"
8. #21 – "You're everything I've ever wanted."
9. #24 – "I'll always be there for you."
10. #27 – "It's my passion."
11. #29 – "There's nothing I wouldn't do for my child."
12. #32 – "How can they do this to us?"
13. #35 – "I can't believe they're gone."
14. #38 – "I can't … Not without them …"
15. #40 – "The tears just won't stop …"
16. #41 – "I dare you to say that again."
17. #45 – "I wouldn't do that if I were you."
18. #48 – "Just saying. That's a hell of a way to go."
19. #51 – "What the hell?"
20. #54 – "You can't be serious."
21. #57 – "Oh my god!"

121

22. #60 – *Gasp*
23. #61 – "I don't understand …"
24. #64 – "You can't just … Ugh!"
25. #66 – "Who are you? What do you want?"
26. #68 – "Why can't I remember anything?"
27. #73 – "Go, go, go!"
28. #76 – "You've survived worse."
29. #79 – "You're our last hope."
30. #82 – "I'll do anything."
31. #85 – "Just tell me what you want!"
32. #88 – "Just talk to me …"
33. #93 – "…by my own brother …"
34. #95 – "It was the only way."
35. #98 – "You were a tool. Nothing more."

Watercolor (W)

1. #3 – "They're … They're coming for us."
2. #5 – "What have I done?"
3. #8 – "There's someone in the house."
4. #10 – "Get it off, get it off!"
5. #12 – "I'll kill you!"
6. #14 – "How dare you."
7. #16 – "You're nothing but a liar!"
8. #18 – "We can't just sit here and do nothing."
9. #20 – "What the hell's going on here?!"
10. #22 – "Please come home."
11. #25 – "I'm sure they're watching over us."
12. #28 – "This isn't love!"
13. #33 – "We can't just let them die out there."
14. #35 – "I can't believe they're gone."
15. #37 – "You're lying! They would never do that!"
16. #39 – "When will it end?"
17. #41 – "I dare you to say that again."
18. #44 – "You so much as speak her name again, and I'll kill you."
19. #47 – "Do you even know who I am?"
20. #49 – "Take your best shot."
21. #52 – "What are you doing?!"

22. #54 – "You can't be serious."
23. #56 – "Ah!"
24. #60 – *Gasp*
25. #62 – "Why are you doing this?"
26. #65 – "Please, just tell me what's going on."
27. #68 – "Why can't I remember anything?"
28. #70 – "What are you saying?"
29. #72 – "It doesn't matter. We're going to make it through!"
30. #75 – "Don't you dare give up."
31. #79 – "You're our last hope."
32. #82 – "I'll do anything."
33. #84 – "Just a little. I swear I won't tell anyone."
34. #87 – "Whatever it takes."
35. #90 – "Take me instead."
36. #92 – "… Babe?"
37. #95 – "It was the only way."
38. #98 – "You were a tool. Nothing more."

Writing Exercises

1. Write an exaggerated scene of you facing one of your fears.
2. Write out a scene of pure fury. Show, don't tell.
3. Write about the first time you fell in love, or what you think falling in love would be like.
4. Write about someone who has just lost someone/something dear to them.
5. Write a scene where someone being threatened counters it successfully.
6. Write a scene that ends with something unexpected.
7. Write about a detective who is gathering conflicting information about an open case.
8. Write a scene about characters in a seemingly hopeless situation – then give them hope.
9. Write a scene of someone acting out of desperation.
10. Write a scene of someone summarizing their betrayal – then plotting their revenge.

Drawing Exercises

1. Draw a comical version of something you fear.
2. Practice expressing anger in both facial and body language.
3. Draw a tender scene between two lovers.
4. Draw 10 different body languages that express sorrow.
5. Draw a character with a threatening expression/body language.
6. Draw 10 expressions and/or body languages that express shock or surprise.
7. Draw something that creates two different images depending on how it's viewed.
8. Draw a collection of survival items.
9. Draw a short comic strip of someone in a desperate situation.
10. Tell a story of betrayal with your illustration.

Thank You!

That's all for now! We hope you had fun exploring your creative side! If you did, please considering leaving us a review. We'd really appreciate it!

You can come back next year for our 2021 edition and do a whole new set of prompts, and a new set of exercises.

But in the meantime, if you're looking for something to keep you busy, you can try our other prompt books:

- 365 Writing Prompts.
- 365 Drawing Prompts.
- 100 Character Prompts.
- And more!

And if you're looking for something fun to read to give you some inspiration, check out our fiction books and comics!

For more information, check out our website, www.TCStudiosHQ.com.